THE WORLD

TO

Elvis

Quotes
From The King

JEFF ROVIN

HarperPaperbacks
A Division of HarperCollins*Publishers*

HarperPaperbacks   *A Division of* HarperCollins*Publishers*
10 East 53rd Street, New York, N.Y. 10022

Cover photography courtesy of the Bettmann Archives

First printing: December 1992

Printed in the United States of America

HarperPaperbacks and colophon are trademarks of HarperCollins*Publishers*

❖ 10 9 8 7 6 5 4 3 2 1

THE
WORLD ACCORDING
TO

Elvis

Quotes
From The King

INTRODUCTION

Do something worth remembering
—Elvis Presley April, 1957

Elvis has been gone since 1977—and yet *not* gone.

I'm not talking about the Elvis-eating-in-Burger King sightings or an Elvis-at-a-pay-phone audio cassette. Elvis lives, all right, but in his music, in his movies, and in his words.

I started collecting Elvis "quotes" in 1978, after *Ladies' Home Journal* sent me to interview actress Natalie Wood. When Elvis went to

Hollywood in 1956 to make his first film, eighteen-year-old Natalie was understandably anxious to meet him, and a mutual friend, actor Nick Adams, was happy to make the introduction.

Natalie adored Elvis, and spent time with him in Hollywood and at Graceland. Unfortunately, their schedules kept them apart, and the relationship fizzled after a year.

But *what* a year! Natalie found Elvis to be sensitive, scrupulously polite, sexy, and extremely intelligent—"not in a school-educated sense," she said, "but in a common-sense way." He also had a droll sense of humor, which comes through in several of his quotes. (Natalie said he got a real kick out of the comment about football, for example, when he realized it also had a musical connotation.)

Natalie recounted many of the things he used to say about people, about love, about music, about movies, and about himself. I began to wonder whether Elvis had left behind enough of his thoughts to make a book. After all, he'd been on the bottom and he'd been on top—both, more than once. That had to have given him a unique perspective on life, love, and all that goes along with them.

Published interviews with Elvis helped to fill the collection somewhat, though he wasn't what anyone would call talkative. Elvis was polite and attentive with reporters, but his manner was usually to put a thought out there and leave it—not unfinished, not superficial, but not adorned either. He also didn't want to offend anyone, and kept potentially controversial opinions to himself (a policy many contemporary stars would do well to follow!).

Elvis was much more outspoken in private, and over the years the files became fuller thanks to interviews with many of the people who had known or worked with the King, such as Steve Allen, Milton Berle, Carol Burnett, Lonnie Burr, John Carradine, Cesare Danova, Sammy Davis, Jr., Barbara Eden, Charlton Heston, producer Bones Howe, Tom Jones, Richard Kiel, Burt Lancaster, Elsa Lanchester, Angela Lansbury, Liberace, Shirley MacLaine, Burgess Meredith, Gary Merrill, Mary Tyler Moore, Vincent Price, Tommy Rettig, Burt Reynolds, Debbie Reynolds, Geraldo Rivera, Joan Rivers, Kurt Russell, director Boris Sagal, Cybill Shepherd, Barbara Stanwyck, Gig Young, and others. These people all had fond memories of Elvis, and were happy to share quotes they remembered. Ditto Kathleen Tracy, whose two books on Elvis and thick file of information were invaluable.

(Note: the alleged seances with Elvis, reported in Hans Holzer's

1979 book *Elvis Presley Speaks*, are not included here. Like it or not, the last thing Elvis ever said was, "Okay, I won't," uttered to girlfriend Ginger Alden when she warned him not to fall asleep in the bathroom.)

Mind you, Elvis didn't always manage to practice what he advocated; like all of us, he had his failings. For example, patience was not one of his virtues, and he knew about laziness because, in his later years, he was a major-league practitioner. This was particularly true after his divorce from wife Priscilla in 1973, when the life just seemed to go out of him. Tolerance sometimes proved equally elusive, and he regularly shot TV sets dead when singers like Mel Torme and Robert Goulet appeared. And though he didn't abide by what he said about medication, he was—contrary to what many people believe—a fierce opponent of street drugs and he helped many friends and associates kick serious habits.

Elvis's own shortcomings aside, his words—in their brevity, and couched in his wonderful vernacular—offer a unique insight into the man, something many of the biographies, tell-alls, documentaries, and articles have failed to provide. As Liberace put it when we talked about Elvis in 1986, "For a person who didn't say very much, he said a lot."

Here—much of it published for the first time—is some of what he had to say.

On Acting, Part One:

I don't believe in Stanislavsky or whatever those methods of acting are called. I don't believe in drama teachers either . . . when you start *trying* to act, you're dead.

On Acting, Part Two:
I like (acting in) movies better than I do TV because—if you goof, in a movie, you just go back and take it over. On TV, you just goof.

On Adversity:
If they knock (you) down get right back up. That's the only way to do it.

On Age:
What becomes important as you get older is understanding
. . . instead of worrying about the things you can't
do anymore.

On Aging:
Take large doses of vitamin E . . . it's good for the nerves, blood, and muscles, among other things.

On Alcohol:
Everything in moderation . . . but it's an enemy. It can ruin lives.

On Ambition
It's a dream with a V8 (engine).

Ambition comes from the brain leadin' the body, instead of the other way around.

On the American Dream:

Ain't nowhere else in the world where you can go from driving a truck to driving a Cadillac overnight. Nowhere.

On Apologies:
There's nothin' harder. When someone does it, I really respect that.

On Appearances:
Just because you look good, don't mean you feel good. Folks *always* look good in their coffins.

On Art:
I wouldn't call any art bad, though there's a lot of it I don't get. I like realism . . . though I can admire a good house paintin' job.

On Assassins:
When someone decides they wanna get you, there's no stoppin' 'em. [But] if they shot these guys right away, instead of lettin' 'em say their say, maybe there'd be fewer of 'em.

On Autograph Hunters:
If you can't take the time to sign your name for someone, then before too long your new name'll be mud.

On Baseball:

I like playin' softball . . . but watchin' [baseball], man—I don't want to knock the national pastime, but sometimes a lot of nothin' happens.

On Beauty:

The most beautiful thing in the world to me is a baby lookin' as pretty as her mama.

On Books:
I love movies, but I love books, too—real ones (*nonfiction*)—
'cause you can reread parts and think things over.

On Boredom:
I'd rather be angry than bored.

On Celebrity:
When you're a celebrity, people treat you nicer. The bad part is, they also tell you what they think you want to hear, which ain't always the truth.

On Challenges:
They keep you young.

On Change:
People are afraid of it, but you have to have it in order to grow and mature.

On Character:
It's not how much you have that makes people look up to you, it's who you are.

On Children:
They come first . . . the most precious thing in life. A parent should do anything it takes to give a child a sense of family.

On Churchgoing:
Believing in God is more important than going to church.

On Cigarettes:
A singer'd have to be crazy to [smoke], and I can't think of why anyone else'd want to.

On Cigars and Pipes:
I like the aroma . . . they're not annoying little stinkers (like cigarettes).

On Clothes:
They say things about you that you can't, sometimes.

On Coincidence:
I never believed that anything was a coincidence. There's a reason for everything that happens.

On Comic Books:
Only snobs who never looked at one think they're bad. [Comic books] do a lot for your imagination . . . and *Mad* makes me laugh.

On Commitment:
It's got to be total or it ain't worth it. And if you lose a little ground, gut it out.

On Common Sense:
There's nothin' I respect more than someone who can tell
north from south without a compass.

On Compassion:
Only a dead man's got a reason not to care.

On Computers:
Computers may out think us one day, but as long as people got feelings we'll be better than they are.

On Confidence:
If you do well, [confidence] comes naturally. If you do poorly, you've got to go find it. Either way, if you want to survive, it's gotta come from somewhere.

On Conscience:

When your intelligence don't tell you somethin' ain't right,
your conscience gives you a tap on the shoulder and says,
'Hold on.' If it don't, you're a snake.

On Coolness:
[Being cool] is knowing how much to let things show, and how much to keep 'em in.

On Country Music:
I think it's fantastic . . . country music was always a part of the influence on my type of music.

On Creativity:
It's followin' your nose [and] takin' chances when you get there.

On Critics:
Don't criticize what you don't understand, son, you never walked in that man's shoes.

When you start out, they say you won't last and when you do, they try and get you to quit. . . . They get you comin' and goin'.

Only babies call people names.

On Curiosity:
Curiosity is . . . the headlight that keeps us from losin' our way.

On Death [see Reincarnation]:
Death is the hardest thing for anyone to accept [but] you've got to.
Otherwise you'll live in fear of it.

It's gonna find you regardless of how good you are. When it's your time,
the Lord's gonna take you.

On the Death Penalty:

I don't know if it ever stopped anyone from killin', but it stops 'em from killin' again.

On Devotion:

Girl fans would throw their handkerchiefs at me and I'd blow my nose on 'em and toss 'em right back and them ladies would hug their hankies to their breasts and never wash 'em . . . that's devotion.

On Dieting:

Man, it's the hardest thing in the world . . . the input has to be as great as the energy going out.

On Dignity:
If you have inner peace, it shows outwardly as dignity.

On Divorce:
Sad thing is . . . you can still love someone and be wrong for them.

On Doctors:
They're the princes of our society . . . the healers.

On Dogs:
Dogs love you no matter how much you do or don't have. You can count on them more than you can count on most people—they don't leave you like some people do.

On Dreams:
They tell us truths that we've got to be smart enough to interpret.

On Driving:
I love it, man. When you're behind the wheel, you're in charge of everything that's goin' on and you're free to just *go*.

On Education:
You learn by reading and by listening. I never met anyone
who learned by talking.

On Effort:
Take the time to do a thing right. Otherwise, why do it?

On Ego:
You let your head get too big, it'll break your neck.

On Elvis [1969]:
My name's got 'evils' and 'lives.' It's probably better not to wonder too much about it.

**On Elvis [introducing his song
"Are You Lonesome Tonight" in 1977]:**
I am, and I was.

On Envy:

Envy someone an' it pulls you down. Admire them and it builds you up. Which makes more sense?

On Exercise:

It's hard [but] after thirty-five, man, you don't do enough of it and there'll be enough for two of you.

On Experimentation:

You don't try something, you don't know for sure if it's any good. Just know where to draw the line.

On Eyes:

A person's eyes tell you more than their words.

On Fads:
Somethin' can be real interestin' or different when it starts
out, but if it can't change it's gonna die out like Hula Hoops,
or slow down a lot, like Silly Putty.

On Failure:
No shame in it if you tried your best. As a wise man once said, 'That's the way the mop flops.' [Elvis was quoting himself from the movie *Jailhouse Rock*.]

On Fame [1965]:
When you're the top gunslinger in town everyone takes you on.

On Fame [1977]:
I'm sort of getting tired of being Elvis Presley.

43

On Family:
You do whatever you have to for your kin.

On Fate:
Sometimes I think everything's planned out . . . and other times, when I think of a little baby sufferin', I think, 'This can only be *our* doing.'

On Fatherhood:
You realize you're not a kid anymore. You have to
grow up fast.

On Fear:
It's okay to feel it, just don't show it.

On Fighting [1956]:
I'm a lover, not a fighter.

On Fighting [1970]:
If a cause is just, you fight for it . . . you gouge out their . . . eyes.

On Fish [as food]:
Even when it's cooked, it don't seem like it. The stuff smells bad.

On Food:
Yogurt and vegetables—I don't know. What's good for the body ain't always good for the taste buds.

On Fools:
Somebody does somethin' stupid, that's human. They don't stop when they see it's wrong, that's a fool.

On Football:
The gift of the gods . . . it's like life in four-quarters time.

On Forgiveness:
I can forgive. If someone's done wrong, livin' with that is punishment enough.

On Friends:
Friends can never be family, but some of the things you go through can make you even closer.

Friends are people you can talk to . . . without words, when you have to.

50

On Generosity:
It's like throwing a stone in a pond, it ripples out.

On Ghosts:
I've seen a UFO, never any ghosts. But I believe in an afterlife, so it's possible. When I'm home [at Graceland], I can feel my mama's presence.

On Girlfriends:
I learned young that havin' a girlfriend was about the most expensive thing there is—besides havin' a wife.

On God:
God is love . . . a living presence in all of us.

On God [trying to fathom Him]:
Phew—it's tougher than a nickel stovepipe.

On Good Taste:
Anything that don't frighten the children is in good taste, far as I'm concerned.

On Gospel Music:
Gospel music is the purest thing there is on this earth.

On Gossip:
Little talk for little minds.

On Guns [see Hunting]:
People say it's a virility thing—but some guns are real tiny, man.
[Shooting] is a challenge, an outlet . . . and a way of stayin' safe.

On Happiness:
Happiness is knowin' you've done a good job, whether it's professional
or for another person.

On Hard Rock:

Man, I was tame compared to what they do now.

On Hate:
Animals don't hate, and we're supposed to be better than them.

On Healing [laying on hands]:
I know it works. I've done it—you can feel the heat pourin' from your palms and fingertips and back in again.

On Heroism:
Being a pioneer is one kind of heroism, but a person who puts someone else's needs ahead of their own is also a real hero.

On Hero Worship:
Some fool once said that only the weak need idols. Nobody said that when everybody cheered Lindbergh for crossin' the Atlantic.

On Hollywood:
Hollyweird has lost sight of the basics . . . they're a lot of fancy talkers who like to pigeonhole you.

On Horses:
When you're on a horse, it becomes part of you. It's surprisin' how *much* you can look forward to the morning when there's a horse waitin' for you.

On Human Nature:
I used to think it was a good thing, 'doin' what comes naturally,' but I'm beginnin' to think [human nature] is the low watermark we have to try and get above.

On Hunting [see Guns]:
I don't like shootin' at animals. They got young ones, too . . . there's better ways of gettin' meat.

On the Ideal Girl:
Female, sir.

On Image:
The image is one thing, and the human being is another. . . . It's very hard to live up to an image.

On Imagination:
Someone who's got imagination will never be behind the crowd.

On Improvement:
The best stays the best by constantly getting better.

On Independence:
Make your money doin' it their way, if you have to, then do what you want.

On Individuality:
Don't be like nobody else or you'll be livin' a lie, and that ain't livin'.

On Innocence:
Innocence lets you dream.

On Instincts:
Trust your gut—it doesn't know how to lie.

On Intellectuals:

Most bite off more than they can chew, but aren't smart enough to realize it. Intellectuals . . . bring dissension and envy and jealousy.

On Jesus:

Put yourself in a situation that's sinful, then do what He would have done. You'll understand what He was about.

On Jogging:
I think it's great for you in the same way that a cold shower's great for you, but there's better ways of achievin' the same goal.

On Laughter:
It's pure freedom, like being a kid again.

On Lawyers:
I pay them to protect me, I still get sued. So what's the good?

On Laziness [late 1950s]:

When I don't do a good job, I know it and I'm blue as hell. You'll pardon my language, but I mean it.

On Laziness [1973]:

It takes more effort to get goin' again than it does to go without stoppin'.

On Life:
Life and living aren't the same thing. Life is more than just drawin' breath.

It don't take long to figure it out. It really isn't that complicated.

On Love:

Love is what makes a crowd disappear when you're with someone.

There's different kinds of love—for a child, a parent, a wife, a pet, a home, all kinds—and the only bad one I ever saw was self-love.

Love is [like] when you pull into a service station and know that you don't want to go any farther . . . that you can be happy right there.

On Loyalty:

Loyalty is the most important thing you can give someone. Truth, trust, friendship, and very often love all depend on it.

On Luck:

If you're willing to accept good luck, you have to be willing to accept some bad luck too.

On Makeup [on a woman]:
I like a lot of makeup. It defines . . . a woman's features . . .
enhances beauty.

On Male Sex Appeal:
Girls go for a guy who is . . . sullen . . . broodin' . . . somethin' of
a menace.

On Manners:
Somebody once called me a sissy for being polite, but it isn't true. There's a 'man' in 'manners.'

On Marriage:
Wait. Wait and find out if this person is really what you want. True love will survive the wait.

Always take that extra few minutes to leave your home in order. Take the time with your wife. Don't take her for granted.

It's hard to put the two, marriage and the career, together . . . it's best to be honest up front, which is more important to you.

THE WORLD ACCORDING TO ELVIS

On Martial Arts:
It's not just self defense, it's about . . . self control, body discipline, mind discipline . . . and breathing techniques. It involves yoga. It involves meditation. It's an art, not a sport.

On Meat:
I like it well done. Cooked. I ain't orderin' a pet.

On the Media:
Too many of these guys ain't reporters, they're marksmen.

One of my guys said, 'You get a bunch of reporters together, and what you got is a co-media.'

On Medication:
No medicine in the world is as strong as healing from within.

On Meetings:
Waste of time. One guy's usually callin' the shots, and everybody else just wants to try and look good.

On Memories:

They cut both ways. There's no way to forget the worst pain,
but nothin' gives you the same kind of pleasure as
rememberin' your greatest happiness.

On Men:
You do a man's work, doesn't mean you're a man.

There's no such thing as a man . . . just a little boy wearin' a man's body.

On Merchandising:
You can't make what the people don't want. And if they
want it, why not give it to 'em?

On Military Life [the bad side]:
You can't breathe or even go to the bathroom without them knowin'
about it. . . . I never hated anything so much in my life as I have the
army.

On Military Life [the good side]:
It's an excellent experience. It lets you find out how other people think
and live.

On Money:
I think, sometimes, it's shameful for one person to have so much.
Doesn't seem quite right. But certain professions are the mother lode,
and that's just the way it is.

Sharing money is what gives it its value.

Money is somethin' people don't mind being woken up in the middle of
the night for.

On Morality:
Do what's right for you, as long as it don't hurt no one.

[Morality is] a state somewhere closer to doin' nothin' than to doin' everything.

On Mortality:
When you look at a body, you realize how temporary it all is, how it could end in a matter of seconds.

On Mothers:
You must be true to yourself. But above all . . . you must honor and love your mother.

On Movies:
Only thing worse than watchin' a bad movie is bein' in one.

On Music:
Music should be something that makes you gotta move, inside or
outside.

Without a song, the day will never end.

On Musicals:
I feel like an . . . idiot breaking into a song while I'm talking to some chick on a train.

On National Leaders:
They're smooth, but most of them . . . ain't got manners any better than the sharecroppers back home.

On Nervousness:

Nothin' wrong with your knees shakin'. When I first . . .
shook, it was half nervousness, half movin' to the beat . . .
and look what it did for me.

On Newspapers:
My daddy once said that the only thing newspapers care about is selling newspapers. I believe that is mostly true.

On Nicknames:
They're real powerful; they can hurt or they can tie you to people in an affectionate way.

On the Night:
The world is more alive at night. It's like God ain't lookin'. . .

On Obsessions:
If you like something, what's so bad about doin' a lot of it? You never know when it's going to end.

On Opera:
I don't understand it. I'm not going to knock it, I just don't understand it. Just like I don't understand jazz.

On Originality:
[It's] acting on an inspiration.

On Parenting:
The key to being a good parent is making a child behave whether they
want to or not.

On Patience:
It gets better results than impatience.

On Performing:

It's either the greatest high or the lowest low [but] that danger is one of the things that makes it so exciting.

On the Piano:

I can't play but—what, three chords on the guitar. But you can do anything on the piano . . . it's like a small band of musicians.

On Politics:
I don't like people who are in politics for themselves and not for others. You want that, you can go into show business.

On Pornography:
Any man who says he ain't interested is a liar. Any woman who says that, she's probably lyin', too.

On Possessions:
All of this is but for a day.

On Possessions [speaking of his daughter]:
I would like her to remember, and be remembered for, the lady she will become, not for what she'll acquire.

On Poverty:
Poor in money don't necessarily mean poor in character.

On Power:
Someone who uses his position to mistreat others won't have that
position for long.

On Prayer:
Sometimes it's good to get a few words out, no matter if anyone's listening . . . just to put yourself on your knees.

On Preachers [denouncing rock and roll]:
Don't run people into the ground for having a nice time.

On Prejudice:
Everybody comes from the same source. If you hate another human
being, you're hating part of yourself.

I hire somebody based on their talent, and associate with somebody
based on whether or not I enjoy and trust 'em. Period.

On Presidents:
You talk about gamblers, man—these men role the dice for *biiiiig* stakes.

On Prison:
What kid ever changed his ways after bein' sent to his room? All he did was try harder not to be caught.

On Promises:
You don't go back on them. You just don't. All it takes is to do it once, and you've lost folks' trust forever.

On Protection:
I have no need for bodyguards, but I have very specific uses
for two highly trained certified public accountants.

On Psychoanalysis:
What the hell makes somebody think they can read a book, put you on a couch, and figure you out? I've known some folks all my life, an' I don't know them.

On Punishment:
It's the anticipation that wears you down, so don't anticipate.

On Quality:
You can't fool yourself or the public for very long.

On Rebelliousness:
I think most people have a natural instinct to rebel.

On Reincarnation [see Death]:
I don't believe that death is the end. Reincarnation's gotta be real . . . it explains a lot about why people are the way they are.

On Religion:
Religion is like music. You experience them and they both move you.

I always knew there was a *real* spiritual life, not the way the church dishes it out . . . with hellfire and damnation and using fear.

[Elvis wore a Cross and a Star of David]:
I don't want to miss out on heaven because of a technicality.

On Respect:
You earn it by givin' it.

On Retirement:
As long as you're pleasin' people, no matter what you're doin', it's foolish to quit.

On Rhythm:
Rhythm is something you either have or you don't have, but when you have it, you have it all over.

On Rock and Roll:
Rock and roll is basically just gospel music, or gospel music mixed with rhythm and blues.

They say it makes us hoodlums. That ain't true. It's a pressure valve . . . . I don't see that any type of music would have any bad influence on people.

I don't think it'll ever die completely out because they're gonna have to get something mighty good to take its place.

On Sacrifice:
Nothin' humbles me more, whether it's a mama doin' without so her baby doesn't have to [or] people savin' up for a year just to come see me sing.

On Satisfaction:
Runnin' your own show and seein' it work out . . . that's the greatest.

On School:
Hell, they don't teach you anything nowadays.

A diploma's not that important. Life's experiences are.

On Science:
Science has some of the answers, but they gotta take baby steps to get 'em. I like the gurus who go ahead by leaps.

On Self-Expression:
Whenever you put honest feelin' into somethin', no matter how it turns out, that's *your* expression. That's you.

On Self-Sufficiency:
You can't go through life depending on others. That weakens you. You have to depend on yourself.

On Sensitivity:
Most men don't seem to understand that bein' soft with somebody ain't the same thing as bein' weak.

On Sex:
We're not machines. We need more than the physical act.

If we can control sex, then we can master all other desires.

[The church] can say what it wants . . . there's nothing unclean about sex. A little lovin' never hurt anyone . . . man or woman.

On Show Business:
Once you think you've made it . . . you gotta prove yourself, prove yourself, and then prove yourself again.

On Showmanship:
If I just stood up there and sang and never moved, people would say, 'I could stay home and listen to his records.' You have to give them a show, something to talk about.

If the songs don't go over . . . do a medley of costumes.

On Singing:
It's a way of caressing people with your voice.

On a Singing Career:
You can't build a whole career on just singing. Look at Frank Sinatra. Until he added acting to singing he found himself slipping downhill.

On Sleep [1959]:
It's not like food, which gives you pleasure. It's kind of creepy, like death, if you think about it.

On Sleep [1976]:
I'd rather be unconscious than miserable.

On Snakes:
They're cold, man. They're the only animals I really hate. Even when they scoot away, you know they ain't afraid . . . they'll be back.

On Soapboxes:
For me a stage is a place where I go to work and sing—not to talk about politics.

On Society:
Everybody's nuts. Some of us just see it more clearly.

On Stardom:

A star is someone who, when an audience approves of them,
puts more into what they're doing, not less.

On Success:
It's a trap, man—the trappings of success is really a good way of puttin' it.

On Talent:
[Talent is] bein' able to sell what you're feeling.

On Taxes:
It's a privilege to pay them . . . and moral, too.

On Telepathy:
I believe in it. We've barely tapped the powers of the mind.

On Televangelists:
Someday in the near future . . . the so-called ministries of God . . .
they'll all get theirs.

On Television:
It's good company when you don't want to be with
anyone else.

On Tell-All Books:
People in the public eye are used to having all their dirty laundry exposed, but these [writers] should show some consideration for the children.

On the Ten Commandments:
I suspect they were written by old men who didn't have a problem keepin' them all. I don't know anyone under God's blue heaven who does, though it wouldn't hurt to try.

On Trouble:
There's no escapin' it. I don't care who you are or what you're worth: there's trouble at every level of life.

On Truth:
[It's like] the sun—you can shut it out for a time, but it ain't goin' away.

It's what you see in the mirror each morning before coffee, before you put on the face, before you talk to anyone else.

On the United States:
I love this country and what it stands for. These war protesters . . . should go live somewhere else, along with any others who don't care to stand up for their country.

On Values:
They're like fingerprints. Nobody's are the same, but you leave 'em all over everything you do.

On Women [1960]:
Women should be at home to raise a family. It's the only way.

On Women [1963]:
I don't like any woman who I think might be able to outwrassle me.

On Women [1972]:

What I expect is for a woman to stand by her man . . . not sleep around or cuss.

On Work:
The best thing you can do is get in there, no horsin' around, and take care of business.

On the Working Class:
They're the people with values I understand.

On the World:
When you look at things from the bottom up, they seem more wonderful than they really are.

On Yoga:
It frees you, spiritually, from the influences that are around you.

On Youth:
Being young [is not] a physical thing. It's a mental outlook, an attitude.

On Zealotry:

[The Founding Fathers] were obsessed with an idea and did so much good, while the Commies were crazy about an idea and did so much bad. Just goes to show how important that first step is.